exam(i)nation

exam(i)nation

luke kurtis

exam(i)nation

a luke kurtis/bd-studios.com production
Published by bd-studios.com in New York City, 2018
Copyright © 2018 by luke kurtis

"examination" originally appeared in *RFD Magazine*, Winter 2017. "autoatomicanxiety" and "cold congregation" originally appeared in *let us prey* (2005) and later *The Language of History* (2014). "love in the mourning" originally appeared in *the immeasurable fold* (2018). "autoatomicanxiety" and "cold congregation" appeared in that compilation as well.

Design and photography by luke kurtis

ISBN 978-0-9992078-7-1

All Rights Reserved. No part of this publication may be reproduced, stored in a retrieval system or transmitted in any form or by any means without the prior permission in writing of copyright holders and of the publisher.

"Can the self-absorbed artist do nothing better than examine and re-examine his own boring insides? Must he piddle on canvas and stage? He belongs to a species that may disappear if he doesn't wake up to his part in the whole."

—Bette Davis

"Invention, it must be humbly admitted, does not consist in creating out of void, but out of chaos."

—Mary Shelley

"We may encounter many defeats but we must not be defeated. But in fact it may be necessary to encounter defeat so we can know who the hell we are. What can we overcome? What makes us stumble and fall and somehow miraculously rise… and go on."

—Maya Angelou

contents

introduction   13

i
privilege   19
the protracted arc   20
examination   24

ii
rhino dreams   31
this avoidable atlantis   36
unnecessary windings   38

iii
terror   45
cold congregation   48
love in the mourning   50

iv

buttons	59
the subtle illumination	60
privacy	62
internet age	68
false duality	71
filter	77

v

we the people	83
a convenient lapse	85
these days are numbered	89
action	92
autoatomicanxiety	93
fears	97

vi

rebel rebel said	103
art history	110
no literary cred	115
the dead	118

vii

before we had eyes	123
a grim countenance	126
before skyscrapers	129
life is a tomb	132
the fall	134
memorial	135

viii

fabulous	139
jesus delusion	143
rainbow symphony	147
the gomer pyles	149

ix

this american rome	157
a pillaged edifice	163
a grotesque encumbrance	170
vanitas (without memorial)	174
we cannot see (all that's hidden)	178

about the photographs   183
about the artist   185

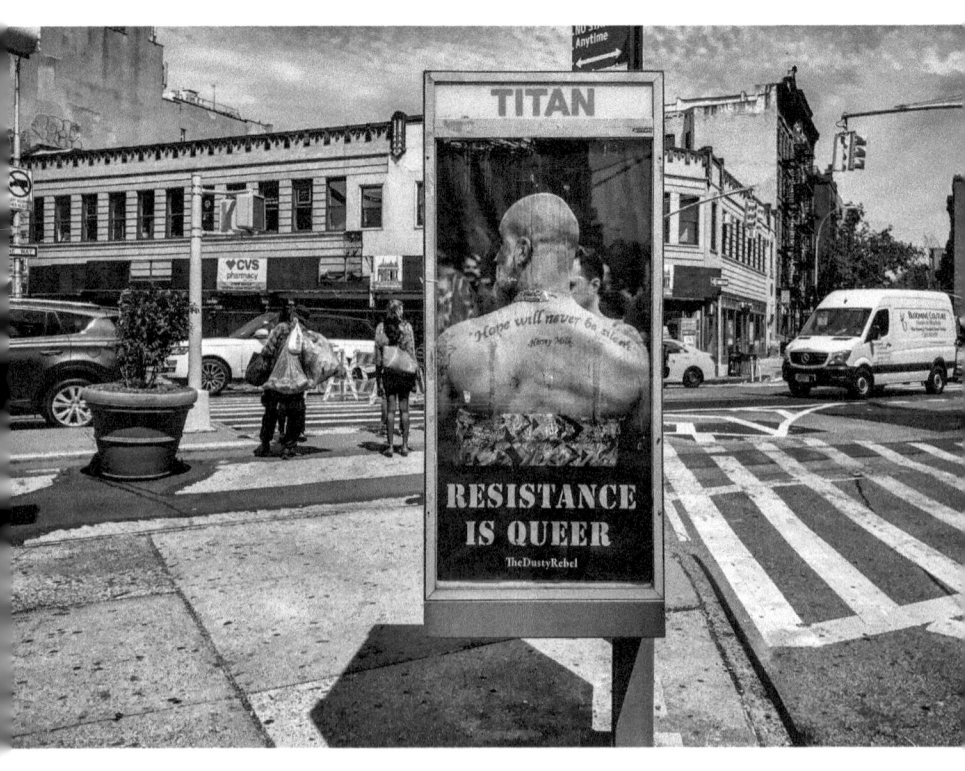

introduction

Poetry has often served as a sort of diary for me. During the 2016 US Presidential Elections, I began to write more and more poems in reaction to current events. Before long I realized I had enough poems to make up a chapbook-length collection. As time went on, I continued to write until the collection grew into what you're reading now.

Almost all of the poems in this collection were written in 2016, 2017, and a few in 2018. I have included a few older poems as well because, thematically, they belong. These poems also help situate the collection within the overall context of my previous work. While I have never thought of myself as a "political" poet, there are enough examples from my past work to show a level of political engagement and social consciousness, even if it has most often been filtered through the lens of personal experience.

I submitted many of these poems to various literary journals, though only one ("examination") was ever selected for publication. One editor, when rejecting my submission that included "examination" and a few others, commented that the poems were "too bald." It's a valid criticism. Poetry, indeed, can be very powerful when steeped in imagery and symbolism.

But the universality of such poetry is not what I was going for with these poems. In no uncertain terms, I wanted to confront some of my subjects head on. My opinions may alienate readers who do not share my views. My directness may make some people uncomfortable. It may dissatisfy those looking for more ethereal renderings of our world. That is fine, for there is no wrong way to read (or write) poetry. If you do happen to think I'm being "too bald", I didn't write this book for you. Feel free to put it down now and get on with your life. But it is my hope that you'll take the time to hear about my personal experiences of, reactions to, and contemplations on life in the USA in our current era. Even if you don't agree with my perspective, these poems can serve as a starting point for conversation and dialogue. Poetry might not change the world, but it can help us examine ourselves and our nation. And if that can be my contribution to solving the problems before us, that is enough.

privilege

privilege is an unknown burden
invisible to those who benefit from it
while glaringly obvious to everyone else

you can't escape your privilege
which is the very point of privilege
you either have it or you don't

it's only a problem when you won't
examine yourself and acknowledge
you carry this through the world

and use your voice against it

the protracted arc

there's a lengthened burden, a protracted arc of pain
lingering in the sky over America like a thorn in the
    side causing pain

there is a violent past penetrating the present
where people speak forgotten language so we cannot
    remember the word for pain

where war and slave incite memory so traumatic
that an irritated glance stirs up so much anger and
    pain

where though we are human, all the same
bridges burn bright in the color of our skin because
    of pain

where we have made mistakes too unbearable to mention
and few know how to reach out and clasp hands without causing pain

where are you, Doctor King? where is your spirit?
where is your guiding light, for surely it must shine brighter than our pain?

what would you have us do in Charlotte, Tulsa, Baton Rouge, Falcon Heights?
what would you have us do across America where our people scream out in pain?

there is a gilded thread floating in the air glistening
waiting to replace the chains of pain

there is a coffered barrel vault above our head
    shining
waiting to house protector and protected with our
    pain

there is a forgotten melody not passed down by
    generations singing
waiting to come together in song with all the voices
    of pain

we shall not pit the depths of our rage against
    ourselves
for we are one and we share pain

i look down at the shore and feel water lapping
    against my feet, river Jordan
baptize the soul of America inconsiderate of our sins
    wash away pain

examination

she came
with a great retinue
camels bearing spices
very much gold
and precious stones

her black skin
gleaming in the desert sun
headdress wrapped
as we liken to Africa even today
dyed colorfully
inspiring poets to capture her likeness
painted in word

the front porch of the plantation home
is attended by familiar descendants
who wipe their brow
doused in southern heat
drinking lemonade
and sweet tea

we pretend slavery is a deed of the past
and excuse our grandparents
for using words like nigger and coon
"it was a different time" we soon
forgive their transgressions

when Congress is in session
and Ms. Warren is silenced
yet she persists

we must resist not just the privilege
marked by our skin
but the privilege of generations before us
who thought Rosa should sit
at the back of the bus
who didn't make a fuss
and march with Doctor King
from Selma to Montgomery

when Beyoncé sang Formation
butt-length braids dangled from her head
swaying like the Blue Nile
flowing out of Lake Tana
Matsoukas said,
"this is a call to resistance"
while the graffiti proclaimed
"stop shooting us"

the music was enough
but the video made it clear
this—here—is what we must talk about
—no—
it is what we must—do—
something about

like the Queen of Sheba
we must ask hard questions

but can we answer them to her satisfaction?

ii

rhino dreams

you told me about a recurring dream
you've had for years
where the last rhino on earth dies

it is an inexplicably sad dream
as you mourn the horned creature

the rhino is a totem for you
visiting in dreams like this
so you know you are not alone

have you ever thought about
what she might be trying to tell you?

last year a rhino in San Diego gave birth
for the first time in ten years
because it was believed she was infertile

or maybe she was just sad
worrying about the future for her calf
i certainly don't want to have children
and leave them to suffer from our mess

there are not many rhinos left in Africa
so this baby is particularly important
a symbol of conservation
a glimmer of hope
that maybe we can care for the world

have you ever noticed how rhinos
always have a bird on their back or head?
in my observations, this is true
whether in the wild or a zoo

today in the United States, we are under attack
by politicians who deny environmental science
for the sake of big oil and business interests

so since the earth is warming like a heating coil
and it appears there is not a lot we can do
to stop it if we don't start soon
maybe it's not rhino extinction we have to worry
    about

maybe the rhino is warning us
speaking through your dreams
not merely that she is going to die

but that we are going down with her

will our birds miss us?

this avoidable atlantis

it is difficult
to consider
the ways in which
our world will change

the islands
that will sink
beneath the sea

the coastlines
that will drown
so many cities

it is even harder
to understand
how we had
more than enough
warning
to stop this
avoidable atlantis

and yet we did not heed it

unnecessary windings

oh! what sorrow!
how the beauty
of our landscapes
pass away so quickly

—the ravages of the axe
increase by the day—

noble scenes
become desolate
with wantonness
and barbarism
scarcely credible
in civilized nations

NOTE: This poem is a re-working of a paragraph from Thomas Cole's "Essay on American Scenery" from *American Monthly Magazine,* Jan 1836.

we park our cars
at sunbaked stations
and behold spots
—once rife with beauty—
desecrated
by "improvement"

why do we destroy
nature
without substituting
art?

this is a regret
—not a complaint—
for such is the road
we travel

yet this path
may lead to refinement
in the end

for when we see
a place of rest
close at hand
do we not dislike
roads
with long

unnecessary

windings?

iii

terror

i walk past a gang of police with large guns
who stand across the way from Stonewall
gathered in groups of four or more

it has been over a month since Pulse
what are they guarding?

#weareorlando is no longer trending
—how quickly we forget—
yet the police are sending guards

is there a threat?
am i in danger living on this street?
if i tweet for news
might some detective assume i mean harm?

where are the guns on Christopher Street?
in whose hands?

the terrorist or the protection—
which causes more terror?

cold congregation

the need for atonement is immense
and your silent recompense
is inadequate

you've gone to battle with
all the freaks and whores
all the restless bores

you've marched against love
in the name of god
for a purpose you call religion

but tell me what's with this
your thoughtless abandon
of ceremony and grace

and how you show your face
is a mystery to me
the way you flaunt hatred

the question of god—of life—
i make no claim
but whether you do or you might

whether you love or you fight
there will be no peaceful amends
for such a cold congregation

love in the mourning

love is love
even if you do not want to hear it

you can exclude, ignore
you can rewrite his story
you can lie and cajole
out of selfish reasons

but love is selfless

love will always be there
even unspoken

love embraces every part of his brother
even the parts he is uncomfortable with
love embraces the difficult pain of loving
and perseveres through the pain

love seeks no special privilege
or desires no special position over others
love knows no rule or law you must keep

love is open to all love
even that which it does not understand

i stand alone this mourning

i have learned to live in the face of abuse
and my heart breaks

love knows a broken heart very well
all too well

love has broken my heart
and i reach out
looking for the pieces

i reach into the void before me
an open hand, vulnerable
i look to faces where there should be love
to mouths who are quick to utter the name of
    love

and i cannot find love among them

but here i sit
an open hand, vulnerable
arm outstretched
and offer my love

there is a sharp piercing
and i pull my hand back
bleeding

i suck from the wound
this taste of pain
coming into my body
like blood into wine
a flood of memories

i do not bandage the wound
but cautiously
reach out to you again in love
i offer the pain of love

in my mourning
i offer the pain

i offer what you cannot give
for i know the chains in which you are bound

but i also know that love can break them
if only you, too, will ride the pain

yet you are afraid of that pain
unwilling to embrace the pain of love

you are unable to break free
and stand with me in love

but when that day dawns
and you choose love
the dew of the mourning
will wash away all our sins

in love.

and i will stand with you.

iv

buttons

everywhere is buttons
for a device
or a screen
or some unseen
smart thing
voices we command
who don't understand
what we say
half the time
yet we marvel
at the magic
of modern technology
and keep her in our pockets
strapped to our wrists
and—never—stop
—staring—
at her

the subtle illumination

at night
when i turn
out the light
and the room is
dark and black

i turn on my phone
with the screen
facing forward
revealing my path
with a dim glow

i know my phone
has a flashlight that
shines bright
making the way
clear and visible

but it's a bit harsh
and i prefer
the subtle illumination
of Facebook
and iOS

yes, it is much
like the state
of the Internet
and the way
we connect with friends

indirect, imprecise
and perhaps unwise
to carry along this way
when we have tools
better suited

but are too stubborn to use them

privacy

privacy
is not the same
as secrecy

my encrypted phone
is not a sign
i have evidence to hide
but merely i'm
human like you

when i was a teenager
my mother went into my files
and read my old letters
emails sent to my boyfriend

i had done nothing illegal
or wrong
nothing at all except
love someone who
she didn't approve

she invaded my right to privacy

"as long as you live in this house,
 you have no right to privacy," she said
"as long as you are here,
 you will do as we say"

fundamentalists use
this excuse to torture
queer kids every day

privacy is a way
to be yourself
without judgment

do you ever dance
in your room
because no one is watching?
do you dance the same
when company is around?

privacy is sound
a form of free expression

secrecy is a way
to be covert

who do you hurt
when you hide
nefarious deeds?
family, friends, enemies
innocent strangers too
depending what you do

secrecy is harmful
to free people everywhere

i surf over VPN
and https
to protect my privacy
—yes—these are tools
criminals can use

but so are guns
and you fight for them
even though terrorists do
much more harm
with grenades and rifles

but since when did
my right to bear privacy
kill anyone?

the government tries
to take our private time
in the name of our nation
they say
"you will be safer,
as long as you live
in our country"

but yet they keep secrets
torture, death—deeper—
than anything encrypted
on our phones
and laptops

this is not
Guantanamo Bay

but byte by byte
inside our own homes
government chisels away
our rights to

privacy

internet age

i am not a poet of the internet age
i do not write verse online to bemuse or rhyme
or find the time to tweet my way across stanzas

i am not a poet of the digital world
sending poems about dusty clouds
of network switches and fiber circuits

do the veins of poetry flow through Amazon's
    servers
crisp ink to the page of lines written
words spoken in diaries of ones and zeroes

<coded> in electronic books, surfed upon silicon
    waves
pushed through filters of democratic commerce
buried in cemeteries under tombstones engraved:
    Mr. Barnes

i am not a poet of the internet age
i do not write millennial yarns of
    microaggression
threading needles of privilege through the page

while the world's hem slowly unravels

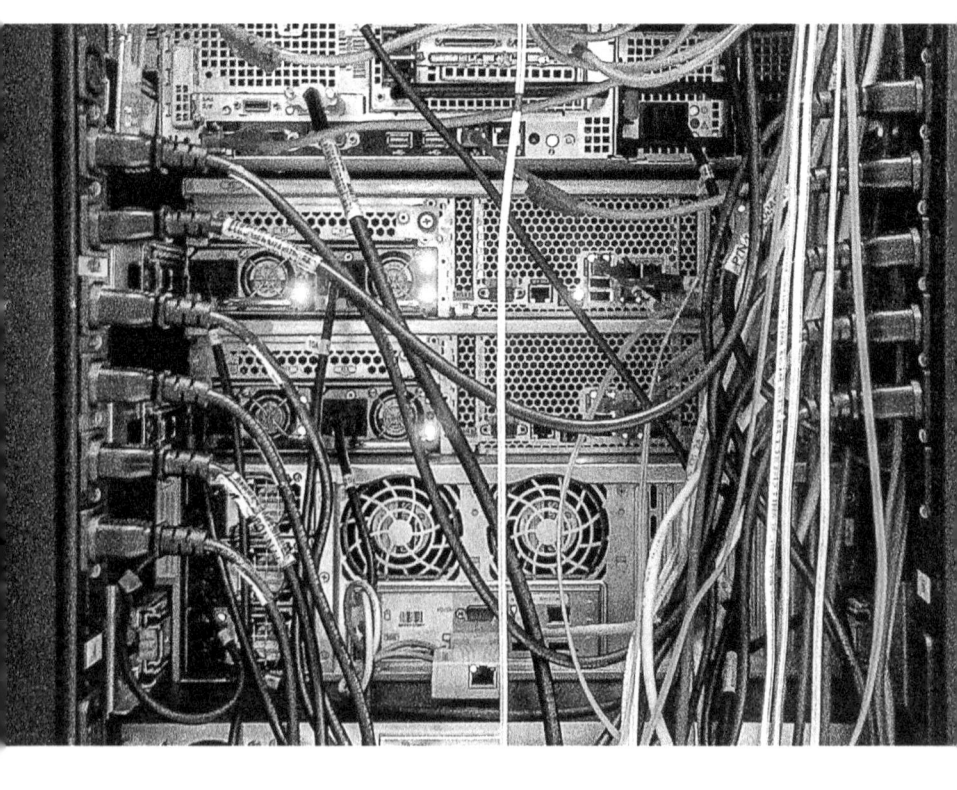

false duality

in the 90s
we surfed the internet
over dial-up modems
and winsock connections

when i checked my email
or fired up Netscape
you couldn't take
a phone call
because the modem
tied up the line

in the aughts
broadband took off
at speeds unthinkable
our pipe
always connected
and we could talk
on landlines
for hours
while we surfed

then we entered
mobile turf
easing us into the teens
where we are connected
in the car, outside,
on the street

and if that didn't play a part
in our fear of the world
with headlines of terror
running across our screens
even our homes
have become smart
with "hey Siri,
turn the lights on"
and "turn the lights off"

at the tap of a finger
my phone can control lights
in Somalia or Congo

how long before my brain
can do the same
smartphone training wheels
no longer needed?

we are leading the way
learning new ways to connect
as technology teaches us
fundamental oneness

we are at the dawning
of an age
on the edge
of a new consciousness

but in our infancy
—still—
we react
in fear
looking for ways
to pit "us"
against "them"

instead of connecting
the world
we are attacking
our friends
imposing our views
and beliefs
from China
to the Middle East

but being connected
doesn't mean
we are all the same

being connected
is a way
to embrace
difference

and make the world stronger

in the 90s
we surfed the internet

what are we doing now?

filter

there is always
—something—
vying for attention
whether in my email
or on my notification list

then my watch
taps my wrist
reminding me to
breathe

see?
i am so distracted
i need this reminder
to pause and find
inner peace

and don't forget
social media
when he insists upon
making it known
how many likes
or views
i've earned

my website is hit
by spambots and
Russian hacking shit
making analytics impossible
if you don't know
how to filter it

it's like my screens
are streaming radioactive rays
straight into my brain
and the more i gaze
into this portal

the more
—i need—
to
dis-

connect

v

we the people

we the people
of the disastrous state of America
in order to rescue our beloved Union
establish resistance
insure domestic diversity
provide for the common people
promote universal healthcare
and secure the promise of unity
between ourselves and those in need
do ordain and establish
to uphold our Constitution
against that demagogue
who wishes to destroy us

a convenient lapse

there is a palpable weight
clinging at the belly of America
clawing the world in diegetic fits
of malignant pages
where fake news hyperlinks its way
across unassuming walls
and the people of America
tap their finger unquestioning

we need more jobs, they say
wrenching smartphone tears
crying, looking for a way
trying to find reasons for loss
longing, blaming the economy
honing in on faith based in fear
to find an explanation

i move my hand
across mother's abdomen
and feel a sharp pain piercing
as my country closes her borders
to people in need
looking for the dream of America
where generations have toiled
through dirt drenched in the blood
of conflict and derision

dark days and decisions
linger over us
even though America has tried
to learn from her mistakes
holding our heads against
the belly of our mother
pregnant and frightened

but we have forgotten
a convenient lapse falling over us
where our yawning insecurities
have buried knives
deep into the womb of our future

this weight, this burden
this intolerable sore
where life has been ripped out
is prone to infection
and imminent disease

America—please—
i beg you to conquer
your fears and remember
why you are here

to begin with

these days are numbered

i would never promise something
i could not keep

i do not like to answer questions
if i am uncertain

i choose words with meaning
instead of demeaning language
and hiding between tweets

if buildings could speak
what would Jackie's bedroom
have to say
these days?

reality tv pumps through the veins
of the White House
dumbing down these United States

oh! the hate spewing forth
makes me ill

they march
with their flags
in the bright of day
—proud—
of the way
they believe

and they believe!
upheld by decades of subtext
from the right

oh! that they might
see the error of their ways

and the imp
who props them up
with what he does not tweet

"how long can we keep going like this?"
you ask

i do not like to answer questions
if i am uncertain

but i am sure
their days
—and his—

are numbered

action

we vent collective grief, anger, and rage
in words and phrases designed for shares and
    retweets

we seek community through hashtags and likes
so that others who listen might understand

so that we might join virtual hands
to stand against the target of our discontent

is this a new spring, a lasting connection
or is it a distraction, a way to convince ourselves

without taking action

autoatomicanxiety

the fear of bliss
is an immense
temptation

isolation is a struggle
against the odds of
extinction

where every distinction
between humans and lower
primates

between man and the apes
becomes blurred and
unclear

a disease of social disability
impolite civility and
death

every step every breath
an accomplishment a
triumph

immense and defiant
the world is plagued
diseased

loud detonation
from the mountains to the seas
everywhere

on land and on air
no place no one is
denied

the depths of disguise
the stoic dysfunction of
autoatomicanxiety

death and propriety
the slow release into
atmosphere

yes—it is here—
this deadly urge for
recompense

and the fear of this
is an immense
temptation

fears

my fears are stiff
crawling out of my mouth
like an anaconda slithering

her scales cut into my throat
like a blade as i gasp for air
unable to swallow

for she would erupt from my stomach
in a violent fit of
incunabular resistance

nor can i strangle her neck
without risking savage reaction
screaming venom at my face

and so i hold my breath
observe this force, this action
that silences my voice

until my mind can dissolve it

vi

rebel rebel said

i used to scrounge
dusty stores
for hard to find tunes
and out-of-print albums

i remember
a flea market
at the church
on West 4th Street
where i haggled
for Patti Smith

and once
the owner
at Rebel Rebel said
"that's an unusual selection"
when i brought
Yoko Ono,
Debbie Gibson,
and the Pointer Sisters
to the counter

"yeah, i like
 a bit of everything"

i've moved on
from discs and wax
for the convenience
of zeroes and ones
and carrying a library
in my pockct

now i scrounge
file sharing sites
instead of shops
to expand my mind
hunting for things
hard to find
even in the age of ubiquity

you see
the cool kids
are into streaming
these days

that seemingly
limitless
glutton of choice
doesn't account
for some of my
more obscure
tastes

you won't find
much McKuen there
Wig in the Box
the Ono cover
cut from *Whammy!*
or that Laurie Anderson LP
with Giorno and Burroughs

and so i tumble
into my crates
making mp3s
to get a fix
of whatever i need
that only spins
on a turntable

when it
comes down to it
it's about the music
not the technology

you might think
i'm a luddite
for saying that

yet i'm anything but
and as i write
this poem
on my iPhone X
i can't help but think

when the Trojan horse attacks

who will have seen it coming?

art history

we are living
a foolish moment
a time when reality
has taken a turn
for the absurd

i have heard
politicians say
things surreal
words unfit
for government

yet they get away
with this shit
running our country
like a reality tv show
prime time spectacle

AMERICAN ART

A Historical Survey

SAMUEL M. GREEN

RONALD

realism in art
ought to be part
of our agenda
to dethrone
this madness

can artists
fight surrealism
in politics
because we
studied art history?

René Magritte
would never let
these fascists defeat
everything
we have stood for

Picasso
would not accept
this malignant sore
festering
in our side

Orwell, Hemingway
would you say
you saw this coming?
did you issue
a warning?

like the Islamic State
pillaging Palmyra
you desecrate
our great
institutions

artists, writers
poets, musicians
we have fought
we have listened
to your excuse

there will be
no more abuse
for our paintbrushes
and pens
are coming for you

we will not hide
we will not be silent
we are building
—resistance—
for the sake of future

art history

no literary cred

i listened to SZA
and thought
she has taken the pulse
of a beat
only a poet
can touch

not a poet
in the way
Warsan Shire
recites her words
over *Lemonade*
(which i praise)

but in the way
she shows us sound
—sex—
and she

there is no
—one—
way to be a poet

i know it is
unpopular
to think of pop
and poetry
in the same breath

"it is the death of the literary"
some will say
when songwriters
win Pulitzers

SZA may have
no literary cred

but
—like i said—
she has taken the pulse
of a beat
only a poet
can touch

and that's
—enough—
for me

the dead

when Brienne of Tarth
says to Jaime Lannister
"this goes beyond houses
and honor and oaths"

her sentiment echoes
my own about Hillary haters
and their need
for a third-party candidate

where is that third party now?
doing you any good?
did you wash your hands
only to sell your soul?

every day my phone
pushes notifications at me as
a child's finger rests on the trigger
between Putin and Pyongyang

who has raised the dead
and when will our walls
come tumbling
down?

before we had eyes

we were all connected to our mothers
vestigial openings in our belly
where an umbilical cord
once connected us to her body
a physical remnant
of biological reproduction
mother's body into ours

where did she end
and we begin?

her placenta wraps
warm and moist
a liminal veil
where only the memory of light
bleeds through the threshold

the splitting of atoms
is a violent act

this trauma of disconnection
this cutting separation
where our lives begin with blades
wounds our psyche
splits the membrane
between us and our mothers

those few months
that in-between state
of past life and present violence
plays out for all our days
as we either claw our way
back into the darkness

or keep searching
for the light
we could only glimpse

before we had eyes

a grim countenance

bodies are full
—sharp—
with illness and disease

beds numerous
with dying

and denying

do you have
no shame?

—regret?—
—remorse?—

NOTE: This poem is a re-interpretation of a stanza from "Man Was Made To Mourn: A Dirge" (1784) by Robert Burns.

corruption
hides in dark
places

but when rays
of light break
beaming across
a grim countenance

you bring
destruction
upon yourself

pray to god
for help

give good face
—warm—
with smiles

while still
—in the darkness—

man's
inhumanity
to man

makes countless
thousands
mourn

before skyscrapers

there are young people
who have never known a world
before skyscrapers were weapons

jetliners stream through clouds
like Slim Pickens riding the bomb

dark curtains billow
through broken glass golden

birds of prey nest
high among trees
soar across air
looking for a kill

dwellings become
instruments of death
harbingers of violence

will architecture
reveal our psyche?

birds fly home
regurgitate food for chicks
who have never known a world

where death was not part of dinner

life is a tomb

we are born
violent
because we are destined
to die

from our first breath
we spend life
hurdling towards
death

struggle
is in our fabric
the moment
we come out

we sleep in the dark
because fate
waits in the grave
a sort of womb

life is a tomb
a fragile encounter
against our nature
to survive

and then we die

the fall

words do not come
quick enough
if at all

while California burns
Las Vegas mourns
and Puerto Rico
descends into darkness

is this before
or after
the fall?

memorial

does memory
linger
in hashtags
and retweets?

are we
quick
to forget
trending topics?

when tragedy goes viral
why do we
measure memorial
with analytics

instead of quiet contemplation

viii

fabulous

being queer
made me tough

i have a
sensitive heart
with a thick skin
to cover it up

when i kiss
another man
it is because
i love

we speak
of Stonewall
drag queens
and Judy

because
it's our history
and our duty
to remember

men in wigs
fighting on
the front lines
in lavender and lace

we stood up
and demanded
"we will not take
this anymore"

don't ever attack
a pansy
we have a history
that makes us fierce

being queer
made us tough
and wearing heels
made us

fabulous

jesus delusion

it seems repetitive
to write another poem
about our country
and how things
are going to hell

but as days go on
things only get worse

Alabama has elected
a man who believes
i should be in jail
just because
i happen to suck dick

well, i don't give
a flying shit
if you're offended
that i give it
up the ass

you don't have the right
to tell me where
i put my cock

how can it be
in the name of
religious liberty
you want to impose
your own sharia
on the rest of us?

you can't regulate god

your religion
is at odds
with common decency

(not to mention science)

that's your own
set of contradictions to sort out

just don't involve
the rest of us
in your

jesus delusion

rainbow symphony

one autumn later
i walk down Christopher
crisp leaves dangle from trees

i pause at #53
—remember—
how our history is laced

with decayed cries
of hatred dying
clawing at our heels

this is one of four
—long, trying—
years

what is a dark quartet
in the face of
a rainbow symphony?

we won't be made
—victim—
or casualty

you don't want
to attack
us queers

we remember
what happened
—here—

and we'll do it again
if we have to

the gomer pyles

when i think
of gays on tv
and the way
we have earned
a place
at the table

i wonder
how my family
—who disowned me
for being gay—

i wonder what
they say
when someone like
Jim Nabors died
with his husband
by his side?

if only they
had known
in my Mayberry

ol' Gomer Pyle
was a part
of the family,
a grand uncle
loved by all,
an adored
older cousin

no one
would be surprised
if he showed up
for dinner,
welcomed
to the table

but what happens
when Mayberry
is not
what you thought?

your fantasies
have made
a different
America

where it is easier
to accept
difference
when it is not
of your own

when it's too close
to home
you force out
queer daughters
and sons

when i think
of gays on tv
and the way
we have earned
a place
at the table

i can't help
but remember
losing my seat

while all
the Gomer Pyles
took my place

ix

this american rome

what do we believe
just because
our parents taught us?

truth is not
a collective wish
or a dream fulfilled
by pundits and pastors

nor something
you make for yourself

we often speak
"our truth"

what is
—truth—
to

you?

what is
—truth—
to

a nazi
a klansman
a terrorist
a dictator

a president

truth is not
science
(though science
seeks truth)

truth is not
god
(whichever one[s]
you bow to)

we cannot
manufacture
truth

yet it is not
always objective
or immediately clear

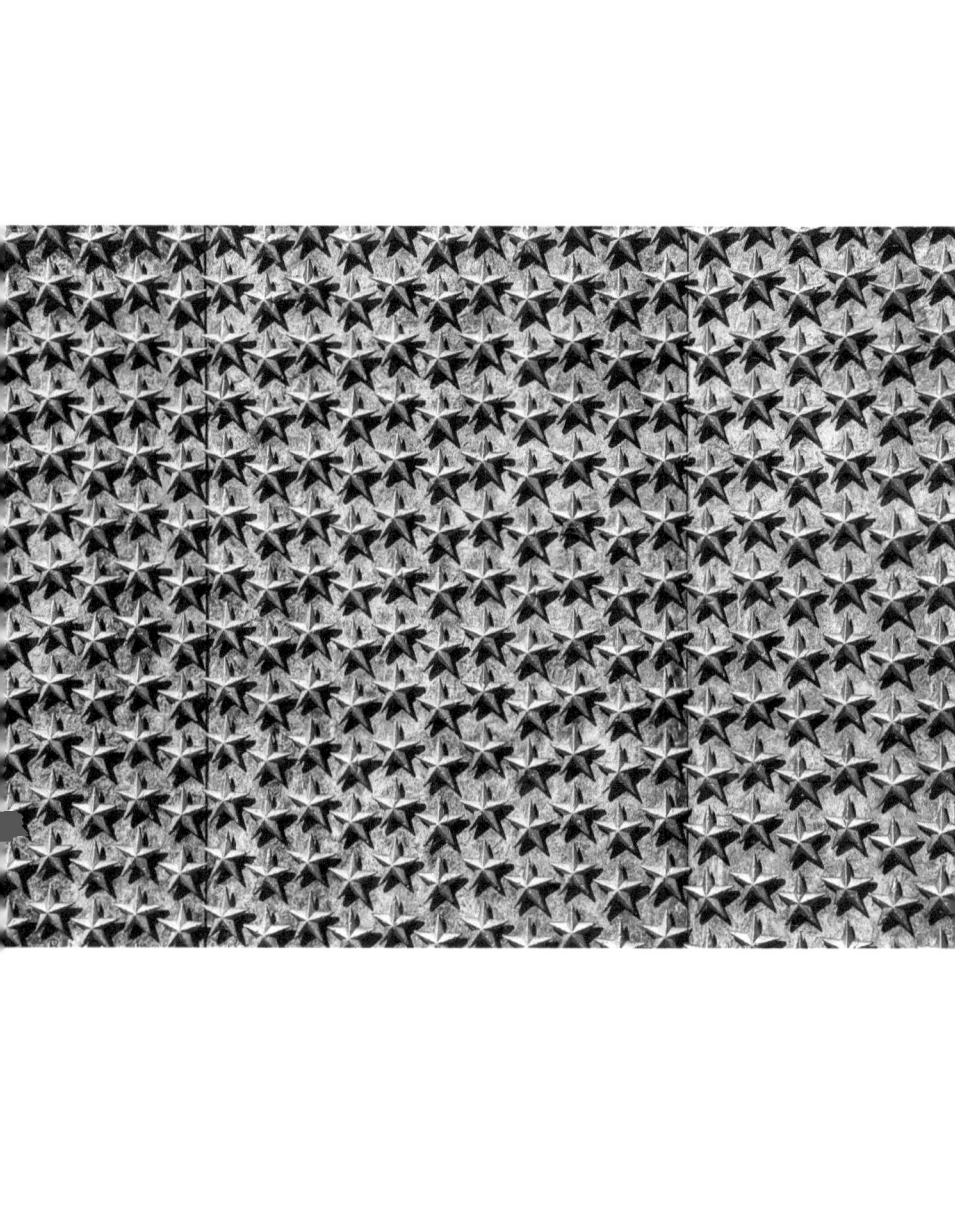

is truth hidden?

or are we
—simply—
unwilling
to hear?

where is truth
in the United States?

is it in the Great Plains
the Rust Belt
Silicon Valley
or the American Rome?

history tells us
great civilizations can fall

but what of our own?

is truth
—here—
at all?

a pillaged edifice

capitalism
beats through veins
across the land
in every corner
of America

but its heart lies
at Broad
and Wall Streets
pumping blood
for coin

art celebrates
mankind
while man celebrates
money
in imperfect proportion

the Corinthian Exchange
is a façade
a portico tacked on
to evoke
antiquity

we memorialize
a history
—a pillaged edifice—
that exists only
within our mind

our statues are bland
colorless
our proportions
orders
without order

our society
is based upon
a weathered memory
—crumbled curiosities—
—forgotten ruins—

the Vitruvian glyph
seeks harmony
between us
and our buildings
our bodies

we build temples
to make men gods
and worship
government
glory and greed

symbols of
this imagined past
—harbingers
of our greatness—
are everywhere

what of
the Doric columns
at Federal Hall
where Washington
stands guard?

shall we build banks
within royal tombs
lining our coffers
with the wealth
of kings?

shall we thread
our towers
with Erechtheum needles
in an air of
reticence and power?

what if
our unseen future
—decrypted—
echoes
our imagined past?

is our destiny
designated
in our architecture?
are we bound
to this path?

or is our future
—instead—
determined
not by our
edifices

but the ideas we outlast

a grotesque encumberance

there is a door
—open—
waiting for you
to enter and writhe
in deceit

a grotesque encumbrance
shrouds the land
as if
—death—
itself has come

a conceited lover
mirror in hand
checks himself out
fawning
sex and desire

are your fingers
—numb—
from coils
wrapped tight
as freshly rolled coin?

somewhere in bed
a hand reaches
for your loins
as you flinch
drawing away in fear

somewhere in your head
you hear voices
that have become hard
to tune out
or distinguish

somewhere in the dark
under cover of night
politicians legislate
in your name
for their own desires

your dreamcatchers
overflow
with nightmares
—memories—
of lovers and liars

only to wake
to the same
—sad—
soul-selling
desolation

unable to escape
or fall back to sleep

vanitas (without memorial)

it is a grisly scene
rendered in dark tones

were this the grave
of a hero
warm rays would
highlight
chrysanthemum curves
in bloom

carnations
roses
lilies
strewn about the tomb

but instead
the wilting air stinks
of a wretched life

deep salmon hues
disintegrate steadily
like a sunset
over haphazard arrangements

he is reduced to bones
—do you see them?—
left to crumble
in the filth of mortality
where there are
no baroque overtones
or gold-lined coffins

vanity of vanities
—all—
is vanity

a fly alights
buzzing through
the careless stack
alighting
on an abandoned nest
of rancid oranges

a skull sits
brittle and still
memory long vacant
left to rot
blotted out
by new horizons

morning rises
in memory
of all the men
and women
he cast aside

we herald a new day

this pile of bones
is nothing but rubble
without memorial

for death has no bride
and we will not

burn candles for traitors

we cannot see (all that's hidden)

i can't wait for
the election to be over
you said

so Facebook can be
about cats and
funny memes again

it was a naïve thing
for you to say
but you were not alone
in this

even now
it's hard not to lament
what we lost,
the new face
of all the hate
we would rather stop

but it's not that
it didn't exist before

it's when someone at the top
stokes division
all that's hidden
under the surface
starts to rise

is it a blessing
in disguise?

for how can we
hope to change
what we cannot see?

bring the darkness
to the light

the light
will make us clean

about the photographs

The *exam(i)nation* photos were not originally part of a series or related in any way, other than being made by luke kurtis. The images were pulled together from the artist's archive specifically for this book. This newfound context, where the images serve the text, represents the kind of examination the author is getting at: how do we relate to ourselves, each other, and the world at large? How can seemingly disparate things—objects, places, people, styles—belong together? Can they? They must.

about the artist

luke kurtis is a Georgia-born interdisciplinary artist focusing on the intersection of photography, writing, and design. He has exhibited work in galleries and alternative spaces around the country, including solo exhibitions at New York Public Library and Massillon Museum. Select books include *INTERSECTION*, *The Language of History*, and *Angkor Wat*, all part of an ongoing series that combines photography, writing, and design. His albums of experimental music include *obscure mechanics* and *electronic quartets*. He also makes short films, including *the woods are watching* and *convergence*, both documenting his installation art projects of the same names. His studio, bd-studios.com, publishes work both by himself and other artists and writers, and he is the co-founder of New Lit Salon Press. He lives and works in New York City's Greenwich Village.

also by luke kurtis

Angkor Wat
Georgia Dusk (with Dudgrick Bevins)
the immeasurable fold: selected poems 2000–2015
INTERSECTION
The Language of History

also published by bd-studios.com

Route 4, Box 358 by Dudgrick Bevins
The Animal Book by Michael Harren
Tentative Armor by Michael Harren
Visions of the Beyond by Stefanie Masciandaro
Puertas Españolas by Josemaria Mejorada & May Gañán
Here Nor There by Sam Rosenthal
Jordan's Journey by Jordan M. Scoggins
Just One More by Jonathan David Smyth
Retrospective by Michael Tice

www.ingramcontent.com/pod-product-compliance
Lightning Source LLC
Chambersburg PA
CBHW051546010526
44118CB00022B/2600